THE
PHOENICIANS

*W*ith thanks to Nina Jidejian, historian and author of many books on the Canaanite and Phoenician city-states, and to Dr. Helen Sader, Associate Professor of Archaeology, American University of Beirut, Lebanon, for their expert reading of the manuscript.

CULTURES
OF THE PAST

THE
PHOENICIANS

ELSA MARSTON

BENCHMARK BOOKS

MARSHALL CAVENDISH
NEW YORK

Benchmark Books
Marshall Cavendish Corporation
99 White Plains Road
Tarrytown, New York 10591-9001

DEC 1 2 2003

Website: www.marshallcavendish.com

© Marshall Cavendish Corporation 2002

Library of Congress Cataloging-in-Publication Data

Marston, Elsa.
    The Phoenicians / by Elsa Marston.
       p. cm. — (Cultures of the past)
    Includes bibliographical references and index.
    ISBN 0-7614-0309-4
    1. Phoenicians—Juvenile literature. [1. Phoenicians.] I. Title. II. Series
  DS81 .M25   2001
  930'.04926—dc21   00-041452

Printed in Hong Kong

1 3 5 6 4 2

Book design by Carol Matsuyama
Photo research by Rose Corbett Gordon, Mystic CT

Front cover: "The Lady of Elche"—from a site in Spain, one of the farthest Phoenician outposts—was made in the fifth century B.C.E.

Back cover: "Pigeon Rock," off the coast of Beirut, Lebanon. Adventurous Phoenician seafarers sailed beyond their rocky coastline and established trading centers all around the Mediterranean.

Photo Credits

Front cover: courtesy of Nimtallah/Art Resource, NY; back cover: courtesy of Carolyn Brown/Image Bank; pages 6, 14–15, 21, 27, 33, 41 right, 47,48, 50, 51: Erich Lessing/Art Resource, NY; pages 6–7: © Ingeborg Lippmann/Peter Arnold, Inc.; page 9: © TRIP/TRIP The Viesti Collection, Inc.; page 10: Werner Forman Archive/Art Resource; page 17: Louvre/Peter Willi/Bridgeman Art Library; pages 18, 63 left: aSEF/Art Resource, NY; page 25, 45: Scala/Art Resource, NY; page 26: Bolton Museum, Lancashire, UK/Bridgeman Art Library; page 29: Bridgeman Art Library; pages 31, 72: Northwind Pictures; pages 36, 49 left and right, 56: © Martha Cooper/Peter Arnold, Inc.; pages 38–39: Giraudon/Art Resource, NY; page 41 left: Private Collection/Peter Willi/Bridgeman Art Library; page 54: Russell-Cotes Art Gallery, Bournemouth, UK/Bridgeman Art Library; pages 60–61: Guido A. Rossi/Image Bank; page 63 right: Photo Manoug; page 65: Elsa Marston; page 67: El-Hage Collection; page 69: E.O. Hoppé/Corbis; pages 70–71: Trip/H. Rogers.

The selection from *The Prophet* that appears on page 68 is reprinted with the kind permission of Alfred A. Knopf, a Division of Random House, Inc., from THE PROPHET by Kahlil Gibran. Copyright 1923 by Kahlil Gibran and renewed 1951 by Administrators C T A of Kahlil Gibran Estate and Mary G. Gibran.

CONTENTS

CHAPTER ONE

A CIVILIZATION OF CITY-STATES

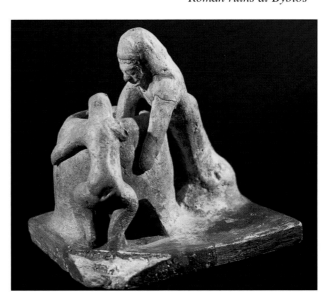

In the Phoenicians' own time, around 2,500 to 3,000 years ago, some people called them clever, hardworking, brilliant, awesome. Others criticized them as surly, fanatical, even cruel. A controversial people, those Phoenicians! But most observers would probably have agreed that they were the most energetic go-getters in the known world.

The Phoenicians (fih-NEE-shuns) lived during the first millennium B.C.E.* in a part of the Middle East known today as the Levant. Their land was a narrow strip of about two hundred miles along the coast of what are now Lebanon, Syria, and Israel. Facing the Mediterranean, the Phoenician cities were backed by a range of rugged, high mountains that made overland

*Many systems of dating have been used by different cultures throughout history. This series of books uses B.C.E. (Before Common Era) and C.E. (Common Era) instead of B.C. (Before Christ) and A.D. (Anno Domini) out of respect for the diversity of the world's peoples.

Roman ruins at Byblos

This small sculpture, barely five inches long, shows a Phoenician woman placing bread inside an ancient oven as her child watches. It was made about 2,500 years ago.

travel extremely difficult. The coastal plain, though fertile and well watered, was too small to raise enough food for a growing population. Because of the geography of their homeland, therefore, the Phoenicians had to look primarily to the sea for their livelihood.

Yet their land was always sort of a crossroads for others: armies, traders, travelers. People coming from Mesopotamia in the east, from Anatolia (Turkey) and Greece to the north, and from Egypt and Arabia to the south passed by Phoenicia. Everyone wanted access to the Phoenician port cities, because they handled so much trade. For many hundreds of years the Phoenician cities were essential to the balance of power between the two great centers of ancient civilization, Egypt and Mesopotamia. Whoever wished to be master of the region had to control Phoenicia.

The Canaanite Heritage

We can date the start of the Phoenician era to sometime around 1100 B.C.E. This did not represent a sharp change from the past, however, for the Phoenicians were not new to the area, as an invading or migrating people might be. They had, in fact, been there for a very long time—under a different name: Canaanite (KAY-nuh-nite).

In the past, scholars' views differed as to where the Canaanites came from originally. Some believed they migrated from Arabia; others, from the west, the desert peninsula of Sinai. Today most scholars believe that the Canaanites, a Semitic people, were the indigenous people who had been living in the Levant for thousands of years, probably with the addition of some tribes from Arabia. The land where the Canaanites lived, called Canaan (KAY-nun), included what are now Israel, Lebanon, the southern part of Syria, and the western part of Jordan.

The earliest Canaanite town to become well known was Gebal—better known today as Byblos (BIB-los)—on the coast of Lebanon. A busy town today, it is one of the oldest continually occupied settlements in the world. People have been living there for 6,500 years. Records and archeology indicate that Byblos was shipping wood to Egypt even before 3000 B.C.E.

From roughly 2500 to 1200 B.C.E., several other Canaanite towns prospered on the coast. The most important were Tyre, Sidon, Sarepta, and Beirut—all in present-day Lebanon—and Akko, called Acre today

Sundown in the harbor of Byblos today. One of the oldest cities in the world, Byblos has been inhabited for more than six thousand years.

and part of modern Israel. Farther up the coast of Syria were the island city of Aradus and the important, cultured city called Ugarit (oo-GAR-it). Most of these towns have lasted to the present day.

The Canaanites were busy traders. Although Mycenaeans (my-suh-NEE-uns) from mainland Greece dominated trade in the eastern Mediterranean in the fourteenth and thirteenth centuries B.C.E., the Canaanite towns found a lively market in many parts of the Middle Eastern region. They traded raw materials, especially

This figurine of the god Ba'al is an example of fine Canaanite metal-working. It is made of bronze covered with gold and silver and dates back to around 1900 B.C.E.

timber, along with oil and preserved fish, and were also well known for their production of luxury goods such as ivory carvings, fine fabrics, jewelry, and silver objects.

During Egypt's New Kingdom (c. 1550–1085 B.C.E.), the Egyptian pharaohs built an empire in western Asia, including Canaan. The Egyptians sought to control this area partly for trade and partly for security—that is, to prevent any strong power from invading Egypt. They also needed mastery over the eastern Mediterranean in order to oppose their rivals in Anatolia, the powerful Hittite (HIH-tite) empire.

For the most part, Egyptian rule was mutually beneficial. The subject kingdoms gave Egypt their loyalty, taxes, and products in return for protection by the mighty Egyptian army. And they needed that protection, because other empires and tribes were always ready to take advantage of any weakness. During one period around 1350 B.C.E., when the Egyptian pharaoh paid little attention to his empire, several of the Canaanite cities were threatened by the Hittites and allied tribes. The unhappy kings wrote message after message to the pharaoh, emphasizing their loyalty and pleading for help. Only after a new pharaoh came to power did Egypt set out to win back its crumbling empire.

The Sea Peoples

Around 1200 B.C.E. Canaan went through bad times. Like a plague of locusts, ships full of fighting men descended on the coast, plundering and destroying. Who were these "Sea Peoples," as they are called? Pirates, marauders, displaced populations, or poor, land-hungry tribes? Little is known for certain—and scholars are still debating the question.

The Sea Peoples apparently included several different groups. Most seem to have migrated from around the Aegean, the sea east of Greece. One possible explanation is that the waves of invaders came as a result of the famous Trojan War (around 1250 B.C.E.), which had led to much social breakdown and change. Whoever they were, the Sea Peoples caused trouble. They attacked several cities and played a role in the destruction of Ugarit. That prominent city was totally destroyed around 1200 B.C.E. and never rebuilt—a boon for archaeologists!

Off the coast of Egypt the marauders met the Egyptians in a sea battle in 1149 B.C.E. Victorious, the Egyptian pharaoh boasted about it on the walls of a famous temple, Medinet Habou at present-day Luxor. Carved reliefs show the invaders wearing curious headdresses like crowns of short upright feathers. This is one of the very few specific references to the Sea Peoples from that time.

Although some pirates continued to harass the coast for another hundred years or so, others of the Sea Peoples eventually settled down. They mixed into the Canaanite population, bringing their own skills, pottery styles, and burial customs. Most importantly, one large group brought ironworking technology. These people were the Philistines (FIH-luh-steens), who settled along the southern coast and gave their name to the land called Palestine.

Rise of the Phoenician Cities

The period from 1200 to 1050 B.C.E. was one of disorder and recovery. By the time the area was peaceful again, the eastern Mediterranean lands had a new map. The civilization in Mycenaean Greece had collapsed, and Greece retired into a "dark age" for a few centuries. The Egyptians, having lost their empire, had slipped into a long period of decline. The Hittite empire in Anatolia had been destroyed. Meanwhile, tribal peoples were encroaching on the land of Canaan. The Israelites built a strong state in the inland hill country, and Aramaean (ar-uh-MEE-un) tribes were gaining more power in present-day Syria.

With various peoples moving about and new states taking shape, the land of the Canaanites shrank. The cities along the coast, though, became increasingly important and prosperous. In those cities the people turned to business with renewed energy and built up their trade, both overland to the east and overseas to the west. By the start of the first millennium B.C.E., what we call the Phoenician era was well under way.

The people did not, however, think of themselves as "Phoenician." That was the Greeks' name for them. Rather, they continued to call themselves after the names of their cities, as they had for hundreds of years. They were Sidonians, Tyrians (TER-ee-uns), Byblians, and so forth. But because the world has always seen them through the eyes of the Greeks who wrote about them, we shall refer to these enterprising people collectively as Phoenician.

Before long, the Phoenician cities were dominating trade in the eastern

WEN-AMON'S TRIP TO BYBLOS

Sometime around 1075 B.C.E., according to an ancient manuscript, an Egyptian gentleman named Wen-Amon set sail for Byblos. He had a simple, straightforward mission: bring back cedarwood for a new ceremonial boat for the god Amon. Egypt had been getting the famed wood for two thousand years with no problem.

But when Wen-Amon landed at the Phoenician town of Dor, thieves made off with all his gold and silver. The local prince was not very sympathetic, so Wen-Amon found a way to help himself to some silver on another ship. Finally he reached Byblos—but the king, Zakarbaal, wouldn't receive him. For twenty-nine days Wen-Amon had to cool his heels, waiting on a boat in the harbor. All that time Zakarbaal kept sending him messages: "Get out of my harbor!"

At last—after one of Zakarbaal's courtiers received a divine message—Wen-Amon was admitted to the palace. The Egyptian told the Phoenician king to give him the requested wood: "Your father did it, your grandfather did it, and you will also do it!" Zakarbaal had different ideas. He agreed—but for a handsome price.

What a shock for Wen-Amon! Never before had Egypt, long master over Canaan and Phoenicia, been forced to haggle for wood.

Wen-Amon had to wait while a messenger went back to Egypt. Happily, the messenger eventually returned, bringing five gold vessels, five silver jugs, twenty garments of fine linen, five hundred rolls of papyrus, five hundred cowhides, five hundred ropes, twenty bags of lentils, and thirty baskets of fish (salted, no doubt). At last Zakarbaal was pleased. He ordered his men to cut some trees and load them on a ship. "Now get going," he told Wen-Amon.

Who should turn up at that point but the notorious Tjekker pirates, masters of the sea along that coast. Knowing they would not let him depart with his cargo, Wen-Amon sat down and wept. More afraid of the Tjekker than of Egypt, Zakarbaal told the pirates to let Wen-Amon depart—and then capture him on the high seas.

Somehow Wen-Amon evaded the Tjekker pirates—only to be caught in a storm and cast on the shores of Cyprus, where he was nearly murdered. He escaped again, sought refuge with the princess of the city, and then . . .

The ancient manuscript ends there. Presumably Wen-Amon did manage to get back to Egypt and report his misadventures. The story tells us much about Egypt's loss of power and prestige at that time, and about the new independence—and arrogance—of the Phoenician city-states. We can also get an idea of goods that were considered valuable, some for the Phoenician market and some, such as papyrus, possibly for trading with other places.

Mediterranean. Far and wide, they were regarded with both admiration and envy.

Even at the height of their power, however, there was no unity among them. For a while Sidon and Tyre formed one kingdom, but no unified state of "Phoenicia" ever existed. Instead, the cities remained independent city-states, as in Canaanite times. Each had its own hereditary king and ruling body of notables, mostly wealthy merchants. Each had its own fleet of trading vessels and fighting ships, and each maintained its own defenses. Sometimes the city-states cooperated, but more often they opposed one another. Later, when foreign armies came to conquer the land, some Phoenician cities helped the invaders against their sister cities. The Phoenician cities existed by means of trade, after all—and trade is a highly competitive occupation.

For a few hundred years, from about 1150 to 900 B.C.E., there were no superpowers to seriously threaten the safety of Phoenicia. Nor were the Phoenician cities ever a military threat to others, since they focused all their energies on trade and crafts. Rather, they maintained good relations with their neighbors and served a very useful purpose as producers, merchants, and middlemen for the trade of others.

Tyre, the Jewel of Cities

After the destruction of Ugarit around 1200 B.C.E. and the later decline of Byblos, cities farther south took first place: Sidon and then Tyre. By the mid-tenth century B.C.E. the history of Phoenicia became largely the history of Tyre. The other cities dropped to second rank.

The sarcophagus on which this trading vessel was carved probably belonged to a wealthy merchant in Sidon, late in the Phoenician era.

This remarkable city of Tyre was built on a small, rocky island a short distance from shore. Before the thirteenth century B.C.E., when cisterns became more practical, the Tyrians had to bring water in boats from springs on the mainland. The shortage of water, however, did not stop Tyre from becoming an extremely valuable piece of real estate. With two excellent harbors and great fleets of ships, it was master of the seas for three hundred years. With its high, strong walls, it could easily withstand attack from land.

In the tenth and ninth centuries B.C.E., Tyre developed close ties with the growing kingdom of the Israelites, a short distance to the south. Israel controlled the main trade routes by land between the Red Sea and Syria, and Tyre was allowed access to these routes. Farther inland, the Tyrian merchants did business with the Aramaean kingdoms around Damascus in Syria. They were only too happy to pay transit fees over the mountains in return for brisk trade in luxury goods.

Phoenicians Abroad

The Phoenicians' trading ventures took them farther and farther away from their homeland. In the eighth century B.C.E., when the Greeks became active once again and dominated trade in the Aegean region, the Phoenicians had to look elsewhere. They headed farther west. Soon they were sending ships all over the Mediterranean and founding "way stations" and colonies from one end of the Mediterranean to the other. Kition (now Larnaka) in Cyprus was Tyre's first important colony and served to launch other voyages of exploration and settlement. As one ancient writer noted, Tyre had an "over-abundance of young men," which gave added reason for adventuring to distant places.

The most famous colony was Carthage (KAR-thij), whose history and culture will be discussed separately. Other well-known Mediterranean cities that started as Phoenician trading stations or colonies include Cádiz in Spain, Bizerte in Tunisia, and Palermo in Sicily. The settlers chose coastal locations with a good water supply and protection for harbors— like their cities at home.

But peaceful years could not last forever. Not only was Greece now a strong competitor with the Phoenician traders, but to the east in Mesopotamia, powerful empires were rising with ambitions of conquest.

Armies from the East

After a time of weakness from internal warfare, the long-lived empire of the Assyrians in northern Mesopotamia burst forth with renewed vigor. Needing access to the sea and the products of the Levant, and enthusiastic for warfare, the Assyrians swept over the land around 875 B.C.E.

The Phoenician cities wisely yielded. For the next two centuries, they were allowed to continue in business, so long as they acknowledged Assyria's supremacy. They paid tribute in goods such as cedarwood, gold and silver, iron, carved ivory, purple cloth—and monkeys, two kinds. It was partly to fill Assyria's demands that the Tyrians had to search out more overseas markets and sources of valuable metals. Although the Assyrians besieged Tyre more than once, on the whole the Phoenicians prospered under their foreign overlords.

Eventually the Assyrians' empire weakened, and they had to give up their hold on the Levant. In 612 B.C.E. their capital Nineveh collapsed before the new power: Babylon. The Babylonian armies under King Nebuchadrezzar then turned toward the Levant, capturing Jerusalem and next heading for Tyre. For thirteen years, from 585 to 572 B.C.E., Nebuchadrezzar besieged the island fortress of Tyre without being able to conquer it. Tyre was badly weakened, however, since it could not carry on trade as usual, and had to yield to Babylonian control. Meanwhile, Sidon became more powerful.

Less than forty years later, along came another dynamic new empire, this time from Persia (Iran). By 538 B.C.E. the Persians had gained control of the Phoenician cities, which willingly became part of the Persian empire. Treated more

From the Canaanite city of Ugarit, a slim figure with large eyes appears to be sitting. Made of bronze, the statue is nearly four thousand years old.

A relief found in the ruins of a palace in Iran shows Phoenicians bringing tribute to the Persian king.

like allies than conquered subjects, the Phoenicians pursued their trade and cultural practices as they always had.

And Then the Greeks

Two hundred years later, with the Persian empire starting to weaken, another empire builder rose and poised to strike. Like the Sea Peoples, he came from the direction of Greece. In 333 B.C.E. the armies of Alexander the Great marched down the coast of Phoenicia. Alexander knew he had to control the Phoenician cities in his campaign against Persia, because the Persians depended on the Phoenician fleet. One after the other, the Phoenician cities surrendered peacefully and were spared attack. The Tyrians, however, made a different decision. Whether from arrogance or uncertainty as to whether Alexander or Persia would be the final winner, they refused Alexander's demands.

No one said no to Alexander the Great. In one of the most dramatic and unusual military assaults in all history, he found a way to overcome the Tyrians' resistance. He set his soldiers to work building a causeway from the shore out to the well-fortified island. For seven months the Greeks piled up sand and rock, while from the high city walls the defenders of Tyre showered them with arrows and burning hot sand. In the end, the causeway was completed, connecting the island to the shore. The Greeks, aided by a fleet from other Phoenician cities, brought their assault machines right up to the city walls. After a bitter defense, Tyre finally surrendered.

Alexander was not merciful. He made an example of Tyre, taking 30,000 women and children into slavery and crucifying 2,000 of the men. Tyre was no longer the invincible city protected by the sea. Henceforth it would be part of the mainland, for the sand that built up along the causeway over the centuries turned it into the peninsula that it is today.

The empire that Alexander conquered eventually stretched from Egypt to India, but after his death it was divided up among his most important generals. The Phoenician cities were drawn into the struggle for power between the Greek rulers in Egypt, the Ptolemies, and those in Syria, the Seleucids. Phoenician trade was also affected by changes in shipping routes and competition from the new city of Alexandria in Egypt.

Nonetheless, under Greek control the Phoenicians prospered and even regained some degree of independence for a while. But the influence of Greek culture gradually proved too strong. Over time the Phoenicians accepted the Greek language, ways of thought, art, and religion, and they became part of the Hellenistic world. Then, it was the turn of the Romans. As part of the Roman empire, Phoenician cities continued to flourish. But as a distinct people, the Phoenicians' place in history was fading.

CARTHAGE

Carthage, the daughter of Tyre, was founded on the coast of what is now Tunisia, probably in the late ninth or early eighth century B.C.E. Unlike the other Phoenician colonies, which started as trading posts, Carthage was settled by people from the aristocratic class of Tyre. Apparently they had left the mother city because of political conflicts.

The name Carthage could be called commonplace: it comes from two Phoenician words meaning simply "new city." But the Carthaginians made sure that their "new city" would leave a mark on history. While they kept up religious connections with the mother city, Tyre, they soon took an independent course. Carthaginian history and culture became known by a different name: Punic, from *Poenus*, the Latin form of "Phoenician."

ELISSA AND THE OX HIDE

Elissa, princess of Tyre, had family problems. Her brother, King Pygmalion, had arranged the murder of her husband for his wealth. Outraged, Elissa and her friends among the upper-crust society of Tyre set sail for the west. First they stopped at the large Phoenician colony on Cyprus and picked up eighty young ladies, who had intended to devote their lives to religion but apparently were open to other suggestions as well.

Reaching a good harbor on the coast of North Africa, Elissa decided to stay there. A hill rose near the harbor, with a fine view; the land was fertile and the beaches pleasant. But being prime real estate, the land was already occupied. Elissa asked the local chief, Iarbas, if she and her group could have just a small corner. Flourishing an ox hide, he answered, "Certainly. You can have as much as this ox hide will enclose."

He hadn't counted on Elissa's wits being sharper than his. Elissa cut the ox hide into many tiny strips and joined them together to make a leather thong—just long enough to encircle the hill. In that way, she claimed the whole area. Iarbas was so impressed he decided he'd like to marry Elissa. She agreed but said that first she must build a funeral pyre to honor her dead husband in Tyre. And when the fire was roaring, Elissa jumped into it herself.

Thus Carthage was founded, supposedly in 814 B.C.E. There may be some truth in this ancient tale. Rivalry and conflict within the ruling class could have sparked the colonists' departure from Tyre. The ox hide story could have been thought up to illustrate the wily ways of the Phoenicians. And Elissa's death by fire seems to have been a forewarning of many more fiery deaths to come.

An artist's idea, based on ancient descriptions and recent archaeology, of the harbors at Carthage. The round harbor was for war vessels and the other housed the merchant fleet.

Carthage grew into one of the most prosperous and powerful states in the ancient world. To maintain trade supremacy in the western Mediterranean, the Carthaginians founded many colonies of their own in North Africa, Spain, Sicily, and the large islands near Italy and France. They particularly sought to control places rich in copper, silver, tin, and lead.

The Carthaginians' wide trading network soon brought them into conflict with another ambitious empire of traders and colonizers—the Greeks. During the fifth and fourth centuries B.C.E., the two merchant empires clashed in Sicily and Sardinia, fighting several bitter, exhausting wars.

Carthage versus Rome

It was not the Greeks, however, who proved to be the greatest enemy of Carthage. By the third century B.C.E. the power of Greece was declining and an energetic new empire was rising:

Rome. From their home in Italy the Romans sought to control the central Mediterranean countries. They soon saw wealthy Carthage, with its large fleets of trading and fighting vessels, as a dangerous threat.

To gain control of Sicily, the Romans fought the Carthaginians over a period from 264 to 241 B.C.E. This was the first of what came to be known as the three Punic Wars. Rome was victorious and imposed harsh terms, driving Carthage out of Sicily and requiring heavy payments.

The Second Punic War, 218–202 B.C.E., might have evened the score. Led by the brilliant young general Hannibal, the Carthaginians launched a surprise attack on Italy. Hannibal approached the "back way," from Spain. He crossed the Alps in what is now Switzerland—not only with a large army but with nine thousand horses and thirty-seven elephants! Yet the Carthaginians could not finally defeat their enemy. The Romans, again victorious, hit Carthage with even more crippling punishments, including a huge war debt and destruction of the Carthaginian fleet.

In 149 B.C.E. Rome decided to finish with Carthage once and for all. The Roman army attacked Carthage itself, a city of possibly 700,000 people. After horrifying battles, house by house, the Romans conquered and completely destroyed Carthage. The Punic Wars can truly be said to have been a turning point in history, for if Rome instead of Carthage had been defeated or seriously weakened, the course of Western civilization might have been quite different.

Punic Carthage never rose again. About a hundred years after its destruction, the Romans founded a new Carthage on the same site. It was a powerful, rich, and elegant metropolis for centuries, and even today its ruins are impressive. But hardly a trace remains of the splendor that was the Phoenician "new city."

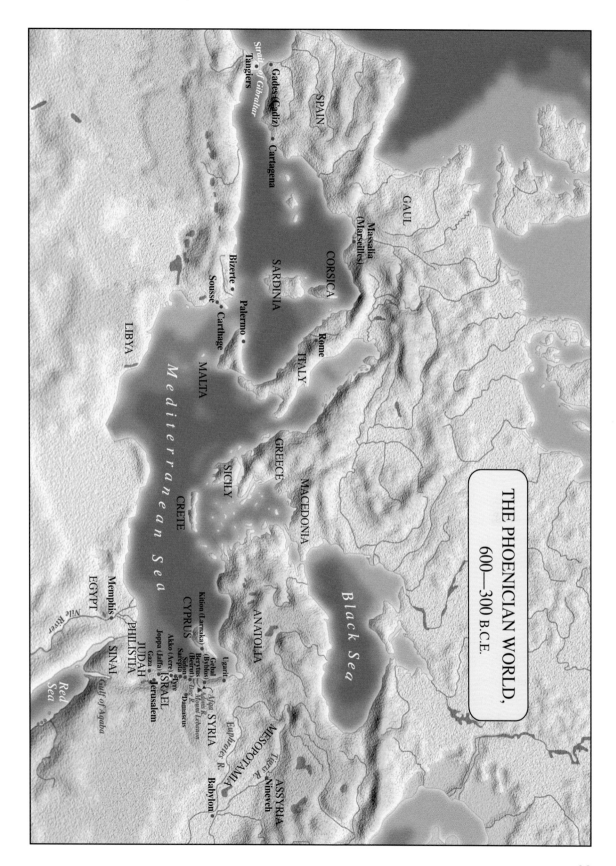

THE PHOENICIAN WORLD,
600—300 B.C.E.

SPAIN

Strait of Gibraltar
Tangiers
Gades (Cadiz)
Cartagena

GAUL

Massalia
(Marseilles)

CORSICA

Bizerte
SARDINIA
Sousse
Palermo
Carthage
Rome
ITALY

LIBYA

MALTA

Mediterranean Sea

SICILY

GREECE

CRETE

MACEDONIA

Black Sea

ANATOLIA

Memphis
EGYPT
CYPRUS
Kition (Larnaka)
Gebal
(Byblos)
Ugarit
Nile River
Berytus
(Beirut)
Sidon
Sarepta
Akko (Acre)
Tyre
Joppa (Jaffa)
PHILISTIA
Gaza
JUDAH
Jerusalem
ISRAEL
SINAI
Gulf of Aqaba
Red Sea
Afqa
Adonis R.
Mount Lebanon
Litani R.
Damascus
SYRIA

Euphrates R.
Tigris R.
MESOPOTAMIA
Babylon
ASSYRIA
Nineveh

CHAPTER TWO

TRADERS, CRAFTSPEOPLE, SAILORS, WRITERS

We call the second millennium B.C.E., when Canaanite culture flourished, the Bronze Age. It was the period when people used bronze, an alloy made of copper and tin, for tools and weapons. The Bronze Age was a time of high achievement for the Canaanites in many ways, especially in the arts. The Canaanites were among the most celebrated artisans in the eastern Mediterranean world.

By Phoenician times, a few hundred years later, technological progress had reached the Iron Age. People had discovered how to smelt and fashion iron, a much harder metal than bronze. Scholars often use the terms Bronze Age and Iron Age to refer to the Canaanite and Phoenician periods, respectively.

Phoenician Arts

In addition to the improved tools and weapons made possible by iron, Phoenician artisans continued to produce excellent work. Far and wide, east and west, customers were eager to have luxury goods "Made in Phoenicia."

The designs and images favored by Phoenician craftspeople show the influence of other cultures: Mesopotamian, Mycenaean, Cypriot (from Cyprus), and especially Egyptian. Egyptian deities, along with many other religious symbols and decorative motifs, appear in much of the artwork made by Phoenicians. The Phoenician designs were a distinctive blend of artistic ideas, however, rather than mere copies of other cultures' art.

An excellent example—though the scene is violent—of the ivory carvings for which the Phoenicians were famous

This ivory carving featuring Egyptian figures and designs was probably made by Phoenician artisans working in Assyria between 800 and 600 B.C.E.

The Phoenicians did not leave anything like the fine sculpture, monumental architecture, and painting of the Egyptians, Mesopotamians, and Greeks. Their artisans usually worked on a small scale, producing things for trade. Ivory carving was one of their most renowned arts. Besides fancy boxes and other small embellished objects such as combs and spoons, most of the ivory was carved as panels for decorating palace walls and furniture. An elegant bed made of cedarwood from Lebanon and decorated with panels of Phoenician-carved ivory—that was the last word in luxurious living!

Artistic metalwork was another Phoenician line, especially large, heavily engraved silver bowls, along with bronze mirrors, daggers and swords, and figurines. Phoenician artisans were also famous for wood-working; fine furniture made an important trade item. Although glass-making had been discovered much earlier, the Phoenicians took artistic glassware to a new high, thanks to the special qualities of the sand found on Phoenician beaches. They produced, for example, delicate bottles of blown glass with bands of different colors. Expensive fabrics and embroidered garments were other sought-after luxuries "Made in Phoenicia," but none have survived for us to judge their quality.

Phoenician artisans were so highly regarded that they sometimes were taken forcibly to distant cities. When Assyria was dominating the

These glass pendants of men with large eyes and beards were found in Carthage, but they may have been made in Sidon. Like most of the Phoenician artwork that has survived through the years, they are small – only two inches high.

Levant, the conquerors transported Phoenician craftspeople to work in Assyrian palaces.

Purple of Tyre and Cedar of Lebanon

Above all, the Phoenicians were known in their time—and are remembered today—for two special products. One was their celebrated purple dye, used for fine fabrics. The dye, ranging from pink to crimson to deep purple, came from a small shellfish called the murex. These marine snails grew plentifully on the coast, but it took a great many of them—and a long, complicated process—to produce much dye. Therefore the dye was very costly, which made it seem all the more desirable to kings and nobles. Furthermore, it never faded. To this day, purple is regarded as a "royal" color, harking back to the glorious Phoenician dye.

Most scholars believe it was the Greek word for "purple" that gave the Phoenicians their name: in ancient Greek *phoinos* meant "purple" or "dark red." In other words, the Greeks called those merchant-princes of the Levant something like the "purple people," because of their famous dyed fabrics.

While the dye came from a small creature in the sea, Phoenicia's other most famous product came from the mountains—and was very large. The slopes of Mount Lebanon were covered with huge, spreading cedar trees, along with pines and cypresses. The fragrant, long-lasting wood from these trees, especially the cedars, was eagerly sought by rulers in countries where wood was scarce. The kings of Egypt bought all they could get, using it for their palaces, temples, coffins, boats, shrines, and furniture. Resin from the cedars was also important in the mummification processes used in Egypt. Later on, every conqueror who invaded the Phoenician homeland made off with as much wood as he could.

Builders

Although very little Phoenician architecture can be seen today, Phoenician stonemasons were considered top-notch. When Israel's King David decided to build an elegant palace in his new capital of Jerusalem, around 960 B.C.E., he called for Phoenician stoneworkers and woodworkers to do the job. Hiram, king of Tyre, was glad to oblige. His engineers had plenty

A PURPLE TO DIE FOR

The shell of the murex snail is pretty and graceful.

How did someone discover that the small, pretty snail in the warm waters of Canaan's seashore contained a great treasure? Actually it wasn't a person, but a dog.

One day very long ago, the god Melqart was walking along the beach with the lady he fancied, a sea nymph named Tyrus. As the lovers strolled and Melqart thought about pleasing his girl with some sort of gift, his dog frolicked in the waves. Suddenly the dog came running toward them, blood dripping from its mouth. Alarmed, Melqart opened the dog's mouth—and found the shell of a small sea creature. The dark crimson was coming from its crushed body, not from a wound suffered by the dog.

When Tyrus saw the beautiful color, she knew just what she wanted—a dress of that rich color! Melqart promptly set about looking for enough snails to dye a dress for Tyrus. Being a god, he succeeded and won the fair lady's hand.

The legend, of course, makes it sound far too easy. Great numbers of the murex mollusks were needed to produce even a tiny bit of the dye. Yet the Phoenicians made quantities of purple-dyed fabric for their own rulers and for their wealthy customers. There are piles several feet deep of ancient murex shells in parts of Tyre, and a whole hill of the shells in Sidon. It must have been tremendous work to gather and kill all those snails for a few priceless drops of exquisite color. And the smell was said to be awful.

Once the author found a few live murex snails at the water's edge near Carthage. When crushed, they did indeed stain the water with a brilliant color, as purple as purple could be. Possibly they were not the exact same kind of snail as those used for the Phoenician dye, as there are different kinds of murex. But it was unquestionably a purple to die for.

of experience, for Hiram was already building Tyre into a splendid city.

Then came an even more ambitious project: the first great temple in Jerusalem, undertaken by King Solomon, David's son and successor. Hiram sent the wood and the best of Tyre's workers—architects, designers, stonemasons, woodworkers—to construct the temple, which the Old Testament describes in detail. Because the Phoenicians presumably built a temple similar to those in their own cities, the description of Solomon's temple (1 Kings 6) is about the only clue we have as to what Phoenician monumental architecture looked like.

In return for the Tyrians' work on his temple, the Israelite king sent large quantities of wheat, oil, and other foods, which Tyre needed for its large population. At one point Solomon offered Hiram twenty villages in Israelite territory. Even though his island kingdom needed more land, however, Hiram was not at all impressed by those villages. "What kind of cities are these which you have given me, my brother?" he wrote crossly to Solomon.

Seafarers

The Phoenicians were masters of many sought-after products and skills, but it took another outstanding skill for them to become masters of far-flung trade. They were excellent seamen. Living on the seashore, at locations with good harbors, they naturally took to the sea. With their timber they could build good ships. With the growth of iron technology—and the rich iron ore in the mountains—they learned to make bigger and better ships that could sail long distances. The Greeks credited the Phoenicians with important advances in navigation, particularly the skill of navigating by the North Star.

As their ambition and confidence grew, Phoenician seamen took longer trading and exploring voyages. In partnership with King Solomon and the Israelites, Tyrian ships made regular voyages from the Gulf of 'Aqaba down the coast of Arabia to a place called Ophir, possibly today's Somaliland. They returned with gold, copper, incense, precious stones—and monkeys. The wealthy classes of both Israel and Tyre had expensive tastes.

In the fifth century B.C.E. the Greek historian Herodotus wrote that Phoenicians were the first to sail around the continent of Africa. According

A nineteenth-century artist's idea of a Phoenician war galley

to his account, they set out from a port on the Gulf of 'Aqaba in approximately 600 B.C.E., sailed down the Red Sea, around Africa, up the West African coast, through the Strait of Gibraltar, and, three years later, back across the Mediterranean to Tyre. Scholars also believe that in their search for sources of tin and other metals, Phoenician ships reached islands off the west coast of England and possibly even Cornwall, on the southwest tip of England.

Just as the Phoenicians loaned their artisans and builders to other people, they also loaned their sailors. The Persians relied heavily on Phoenician fleets to carry out their conquest of Egypt in 525 B.C.E. and their wars against Greece. Making themselves useful to the current superpower in the region was a proven way for the Phoenician cities to survive and continue their business as usual.

The First Alphabet

While all these skills made the Phoenicians famous in their time, their most important achievement is one that vitally affects people today—including the readers of this book! We can credit the Phoenicians with bringing into use the first alphabet.

The art of writing had been known in the Middle East since the fourth millennium, but the various forms of writing were extremely complicated and difficult to learn. In Egypt, for example, writing consisted of hieroglyphs, a combination of pictures and symbols that stood for sounds, words, and ideas. In Mesopotamia scribes wrote in cuneiform, by imprinting wedge-shaped marks on damp clay tablets. Different arrangements of these marks stood for words and syllables, and syllables could consist of many different combinations of consonants and vowels. Both hieroglyphic and cuneiform writing, therefore, required that scribes memorize hundreds of different symbols.

In contrast, the Phoenician alphabet was made up of only twenty-two simple marks that stood for different sounds. These were consonant sounds only. The reader had to figure out the correct vowel sounds—as is true of today's Semitic languages such as Arabic and Hebrew. By combining the sound-symbols, the writer could easily create a word and the reader could almost as easily decipher it, whatever the language. Thus many people could learn to read and write, instead of just a few scribes who had to study for years.

How do we know when the Phoenician alphabet was fully developed? The best clue thus far is the handsome stone sarcophagus in which King Ahiram of Byblos was buried, around 1000 B.C.E. Ahiram's son had a message carved on the lid, a warning to anyone who might disturb the burial. This is the first clear example of the Phoenician alphabet that we know about, although undoubtedly it had already been in use for a while.

Thanks to the Phoenician alphabet, many people could learn to read and write. This stone marker was found in the remains of a Phoenician colony on the island of Malta.

Naturally the Phoenicians did not think up their alphabet out of thin air. Other peoples had also been developing simpler ways to write. In the ruins of Ugarit archaeologists found clay cuneiform tablets written in an alphabet-like cuneiform script. There is also evidence of an early script from Sinai. New archaeological discoveries—as recent as 1999—suggest that Egyptians were beginning to write in simplified symbols like an alphabet as far back as 2000 B.C.E. These early attempts appear to have culminated in the Phoenicians' achievement: the first really flexible set of sound-symbols.

THE ALPHABET, FROM ANCIENT TO MODERN

The letter *A* was originally an ox head in Egyptian hieroglyphs, possibly because cattle were such a basic form of wealth in ancient Egypt. Turn our *A* upside down, and you'll see. *B*, in Egyptian hieroglyphs, was a house (with a simple floor plan!), and *bet* or *beit* means "house" in Semitic languages such as Arabic and Hebrew. A delta, the land formed by deposits at the mouth of a river, often shaped like a triangle, is named after the Greek letter *delta*, our *D*. The hieroglyph for *R* is a human head; in today's Semitic languages, "head" is *ras* or *rosh*. *O* was originally an eye; the Arabic word for "eye" is *ayn*, very close to the Phoenician name for the letter. The hieroglyph for *I*, called *yod* in Phoenician, was a hand—and the word for "hand" in Arabic is *yad*. *K*, too, was a hand, palm up, in hieroglyphs; the Phoenician word *kaph* is like the Arabic word *kaf*, meaning "palm of the hand."

Egyptian Hieroglyphs (Semitic words)	Phoenician	Greek	Roman/Modern
alpu (ox)	aleph	alpha	A
betu (house)	bet	beta	B
	gimel	gamma	C, G
	daleth	delta	D
	heth	eta	H
yadu (hand)	yadu (hand)	iota	I
kappu (palm)	kaph	kappa	K
mayyuma (water)	mem	mu	M
nahasu (snake)	nun	nul	N
enu (eye)	ayin	omicron	O
rasu (head)	resh	rho	R
	shin	sigma	S

The Phoenician language was one of several Semitic languages spoken by the various peoples of the Middle East. The alphabet of sound-symbols naturally suited the Phoenician language best, but it had the great advantage of being adaptable to other languages. Before long, the Greeks learned the alphabet, and later the Romans. Both made some changes but kept the basic idea. Although our own alphabet, based on the Latin (Roman) one, does not look much like the letters used on Ahiram's sarcophagus, it is directly descended from the Phoenician alphabet. Even the names we use for several of our letters come from those of the Phoenicians and Greeks (a—aleph/alpha, b—bet/beta, d—daleth/delta, and others.)

But Where Are the Phoenician Writers?

Here, however, lies a great irony. The Phoenicians, who are credited with the first alphabet, left almost no writing! This was not because they never wrote. The Old Testament mentions the poets, historians, and philosophers of Tyre and Sidon. In fact, biblical scholars find in the Old Testament strong hints of influence by both Canaanite and Phoenician religious literature. It's known, too, that Phoenician cities kept extensive records, annals, and histories.

The problem was that by Phoenician times, people were using different kinds of writing materials. Rather than the clay tablets used earlier, they favored materials such as papyrus from Egypt and parchment. These were easier to use and better suited to the Phoenician way of writing. But while papyrus and parchment lasted well in the dry climate of the Egyptian desert, they decayed in the humid climate of the Levant coast. Some records, too, were lost in times of attack on the major Phoenician cities. In short, almost no Phoenician writing has yet been discovered that tells about their society, beliefs, religion, government, or families. Nothing remains but brief inscriptions on stone, such as upright tablets called stelae (STEE-lee) that indicate burials or religious offerings.

A Phoenician priest in the eleventh century B.C.E. is believed to have written something about religion, but it is preserved only in fragments translated more than a thousand years later. Besides that and archaeological evidence, we can learn about the Phoenicians only from what other people said about them. The main sources are the Old Testament,

This stele was found in Carthage and dates back to the Roman period.

Assyrian records, the account by a Jewish historian named Josephus who lived in the first century C.E., and the works of Greek historians. But "outsiders" who write about a group often have their own purposes in writing. They rarely give a very accurate, thorough, or fair account of the people they are describing.

Just the same, we have a picture of the Phoenicians as a clever and inventive people, artistic and intelligent, enterprising and industrious. Their culture flourished for around eight hundred years, despite the alien cultures of stronger powers that came and went—Egyptian, Mesopotamian, Persian. Then came the Greeks. Even before Alexander's arrival Phoenicians had been increasingly influenced by Greek culture. Under Greek domination they began learning the Greek language, adopting

Greek dress, and absorbing Greek ideas about religion, education, philosophy, and art. They enjoyed Greek-style festivals, athletic contests, and pageants. Although some held on to their traditional ways, their culture eventually became more Greek than Phoenician.

∼CARTHAGE∼

Punic culture, too, took on some "new ways." The Carthaginians mingled with and were influenced by a variety of other Mediterranean peoples.

Like the Phoenicians of the home country, the Carthaginians produced and bartered trade goods for the resources they wanted. Some of their trade goods, it appears, were a bit on the shoddy side: trinkets, flashy things to dazzle the eyes of the less sophisticated people with whom they traded. Luxury items for the home consumers were much better made.

Surprisingly, for merchants and seafarers, the Carthaginians also excelled in a very different skill. They were good farmers. On their farms they experimented with crops and animal husbandry, trying to develop improved methods and standards. For this they were admired—even though criticized for their sharp trading practices!

The Carthaginians preferred to concentrate on making money, rather than war. But when forced into conflict, they took on the military role with great determination. Although relying largely on mercenary troops for battle, they built mighty defenses for their city and a strong fleet of fighting vessels. The Carthaginian army was especially feared for its trained elephants, which crushed anything and anyone in their path. But woe to any Carthaginian general who failed in a military campaign: he could expect a painful and humiliating execution.

Another Loss

Still, we know very little about the Carthaginians, other than what archaeology has revealed. Almost nothing remains of the Carthaginians' writings, nothing in their own words about their ideas, beliefs, and practices. The main reason does not lie in the writing materials they used, as was true for the Phoenicians. Rather, it was because of the tragic fate that Carthage suffered.

When the Romans destroyed Carthage, they took special care to destroy or disperse the written materials. All the records of every sort, including the large library for which Carthage was famous, vanished. The only thing that survived was a lengthy work by an agricultural expert, which the Romans kept because it was useful. Today only small fragments of that work remain, dealing with vines, olives, beekeeping, and the characteristics of a good cow. No accounts of the Carthaginians exist from their own time, other than those written by Greeks and Romans—their mortal enemies!

In spite of the destruction of Carthage in 146 B.C.E., Punic culture did not disappear from North Africa. Several other Punic towns existed along the coast of Tunisia and were spared the Roman attack. For about two hundred years more, those towns and some centers in Spain preserved aspects of the culture from the original homeland in the eastern Mediterranean. The culture of the Canaanites, Phoenicians, and Punic Carthaginians can therefore be said to have lasted well over two thousand years . . . a remarkable achievement in human history.

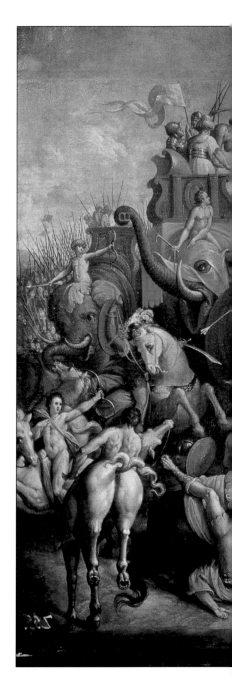

In the decisive battle of the Second Punic War, the elephants got completely out of hand. This is how a sixteenth-century painter imagined the scene.

CHAPTER THREE

The Family of Gods

Canaan may have been a land of "milk and honey," as the Bible describes it, compared to the nearby deserts. But good weather could not be counted on. People always feared drought, as they do today, and bad storms could bring floods, hail, even snow. The Canaanite peasants' life was full of uncertainty caused by nature, so their religion focused on the mysterious forces controlling nature. They believed that if they could somehow influence those forces, their lives would be more secure.

Religious beliefs, rituals, and stories were aimed at explaining and influencing the fertility of the land. People needed a way to understand why the land seemed to die every year and then come to life again. They needed to feel confident that the rains would come and the seasons change in the right way—and that they could do something about it. Therefore they worshipped deities who represented nature, its forces and cycles, its blessings and dangers.

Even though the prominent city of Ugarit was destroyed around 1200 B.C.E., a lot of its written records were somehow preserved. Starting in 1929, archaeologists excavated and studied this treasure. The method of writing was cuneiform. For this we can be thankful, because in spite of the drawbacks of clay tablets, they last almost forever! The texts from Ugarit are the only written evidence of Canaanite religion that exists today.

Nothing similar remains from the Phoenician era, so scholars know much less about Phoenician religion. It is probable, however, that many of the basic religious ideas continued. Nature and fertility cults still held great appeal for the people.

Gods and Goddesses

The Phoenicians appear to have worshipped a collection of deities; thirteen or fourteen are known. Of these, three were usually supreme. At the top of the family was El, a Semitic word that means simply "god." An

At left: *Ba'al as a storm god (Canaanite)*. At right: *A Phoenician female deity wears a headdress similar to that of the Egyptian goddess Isis.*

all-powerful "father" god, El was benevolent toward humankind, but distant and vague. People didn't understand much about him or apparently think much about him, other than to recognize his supremacy.

Closer to humankind and more "knowable" was the main female deity. Sometimes regarded as El's wife, she was called a variety of names, including Astarte (uh-STAR-tee) and Baalat, or "lady." Like a mother goddess, Astarte symbolized fertility and the fruitful earth; she also had powers affecting the sea and the moon. Baalat Gebal, identified with the Egyptian goddess Isis, was prominent in Byblos and had a large temple there as early as 2800 B.C.E.

The third most important deity was Baal, a vigorous young man, who personified the fruitfulness of the earth. Sometimes Baal was known simply by that name, and sometimes he became identified with other gods, for instance Melqart (mel-KART). Representing the changing seasons, he fought against chaos and the destructive forces of nature, such as storms and death. Baal, in his various forms, seems to have been the most popular of Phoenician deities.

Since the word Baal meant "lord," he was often known as lord of a particular place, such as Baal-Shamim ("lord of the heavens") or Baal-Lebanon ("lord of the mountain"). In particular, he was understood as a mountain god whose home was in high, remote places. For instance, Baal-Saphon lived on a mountain called Saphon, rising near the Syrian coast. Winter storms and rain struck that area hard because of the mountain barrier, and this made people think that Baal-Saphon had power over rainstorms, wind, and thunder.

The Larger Family of Deities

In addition to El, Astarte, and Baal, there were several other important deities. Most famous was Melqart, the patron god of Tyre. He seems to have been an all-around powerful, well-muscled god, because the Greeks identified him with their semidivine hero Hercules. When Alexander the Great approached Tyre in his sweep down the coast of Phoenicia, he asked the Tyrians to let him worship at the Temple of Melqart, the greatest temple in the island city. After all, Alexander said, he was descended from Hercules, and the two hero-gods were pretty much the same. The Tyrians declined, however, saying he could worship at a different temple

THE STRUGGLE BETWEEN BAAL AND YAM

This Canaanite myth was found at Ugarit in 1931, written on clay tablets. It tells how Baal, god of rain and fertility, dealt with his rival Yam, who represented the wild winter seas and flooding rivers.

The supreme god El, now old and tired, favors his son Yam to succeed him. He instructs the gods' craftsman, Kothar, to build a palace for Prince Yam—and to be quick about it. Kothar, however, supports Baal, Yam's cousin and chief rival. He tells Yam to expect trouble.

Yam sends messengers to the palace of El, where all the deities are seated. The messengers demand that Baal be turned over to Yam. The deities lower their heads to their knees in fear, but Baal, standing beside El, gets angry . He gets angrier still when El announces that he must serve and pay tribute to Yam. In a fury Baal tries to strike the messengers, until two goddesses seize his arms and remind him of proper conduct.

With his supporters Baal descends to Yam's fearsome abode under the sea. He is soon overcome by his enemy's power, but faithful Kothar urges him to rise and get on with the fight so that he can claim his kingdom. He also gives Baal two magic clubs. Because Baal is still weak, Kothar tells the clubs to leap from Baal's hands "like an eagle." One club strikes Yam on the back, with no effect. The other strikes Yam on the forehead—and drops him. Baal recovers enough to finish Yam off. The two goddesses who have accompanied him proclaim that Yam is dead and Baal will be king.

In this story the Canaanites assured themselves that the winter storms would pass and the warm spring would revive the land.

on the mainland. It was largely because of this refusal that the offended Alexander determined to take Tyre by force.

The goddesses Asherat and Anat had much in common with Astarte but were distinct. Eshmun was another important god, concerned with health and healing. Lesser, more specialized deities included Resheph, a god of lightning and fire, and Dagon, the god of wheat and the plow.

The Phoenicians had no "national" religion, just as they had no "nation." Each city claimed a patron god and a goddess, usually Astarte. The nature of the various gods changed from city to city. Priests sometimes emphasized different qualities of the gods to suit their own purposes or because of political changes. Some political treaties give an idea of the relative importance of the various deities. For example, around 670 B.C.E. a treaty between Assyria and Tyre listed in order all the gods who would punish the king of Tyre if he did not live up to his word.

The Phoenicians also accepted gods from other peoples' religions, particularly the Egyptians. The protective Egyptian god Bes, shown as a grotesque dwarf, was especially popular. Few people in those days felt there was anything wrong with combining deities. As the Greeks started to trade with the Phoenicians, from the ninth century on, they identified the Phoenician gods with their own. In their thinking El became the Greek god Cronus, Astarte became Aphrodite, Melqart became Hercules, and Eshmun became Asklepios.

Temples and High Places

The Phoenicians liked open-air worship, especially in high places in the mountains or beside certain springs or groves of sacred trees. Perhaps they felt that in these outdoor sanctuaries, people might come more closely in touch with their deities. Small shrines were built at some of the sacred spots, and even the cities had temples located on high ground outside the city proper.

Temples were also necessary for worship, each temple apparently serving one god. The king of the city usually took the role of high priest, and he had a large staff of priests and priestesses, singers, and other people who took care of the god's needs. To support all this activity, the wealthy townspeople filled their temples with gold and jewels. They could even borrow from this treasure when necessary, as though the temples were banks!

An important group of Phoenicians had special religious needs: the seafarers. Though brave and skilled, they knew all too well the perils of the sea. Not only were winter storms a danger, but so were the monsters lurking in the deep. Therefore seamen took special care to worship those deities with power over the weather and the sea, and those who helped navigation. These deities included Baal-Hadad, the storm god; Melqart, the guardian of seafarers; and a marine god known as Baal-Berit, Lord of

EUROPA AND THE BULL, A GREEK MYTH

One day Europa, the beautiful daughter of King Agenor of Tyre, was playing with her friends at the beach. A magnificent white bull, grazing nearby, caught her eye. Curious, Europa approached the bull. Since it seemed so gentle and good-natured, she started to caress it and wind garlands of flowers around its horns. Then—the bull almost seemed to beg her to do so—she climbed on its back for a little ride.

Suddenly the bull headed for the water and plunged in. Soon it was swimming out to sea, with terrified Europa clinging to its back. On the shore her friends called frantically, then hurried to tell the king what had happened to his cherished daughter.

Agenor promptly sent his four sons off to look for their sister, warning them not to return without her. The first three failed in their quest, but did become founders of important nations. The fourth, Cadmus, went to Greece, where an oracle advised him to found a city. That city became the celebrated Thebes, birthplace of heroes.

And what about poor Europa? Although she never saw her home again, her life turned out quite nicely. The white bull, of course, was Zeus, king of the gods and master of disguise, well known for his roving eye. He took her to the island of Crete, where they lived happily and Europa had three sons, all of whom became heroes and kings.

Cadmus, meanwhile, evidently had time to teach his adopted countrymen how to read and write—for Greek legend credits him with bringing the alphabet from Phoenicia to Greece. Europa achieved no less, for the whole continent of Europe was named after her. And many an artist has painted her dramatic seduction by the bull!

A serene Europa rides on a stately bull in this sixth-century B.C.E. relief from a temple in Sicily.

Beirut. Astarte guided the steersman and was associated with the new moon, which seamen thought predicted weather patterns.

Before and after their voyages, the seamen carried out special religious ceremonies in temples and small shrines on land. Anchors and models of ships have been found in the ruins of temples along the coast—but not farther inland. While at sea, the sailors believed that their whole ship acquired a sacred protective spirit. The Phoenicians' and Carthaginians' devotion to their religion must have been a vital factor in their willingness to venture so far on unknown waters.

Sacrifice

How did the Phoenicians worship their gods? So far as we can tell, largely by sacrifice. People made offerings to appease the gods and keep them in a benevolent humor, hoping that the gods would allow good things to happen, keep people safe, and avert danger. Believing that the gods were responsible for whatever good came their way, they also made vows and sacrifices in gratitude. In incense-perfumed ceremonies, people gave the temple such things as jewelry, glass perfume bottles, coins, and statuettes.

The Phoenician deities also had a taste for good food. "Price lists" for sacrifices have been found in Carthage and in the ruins of a Punic colony at Marseilles, France. These lists may also give an idea of the way sacrifices were handled in the homeland. Individuals would pay the priests certain amounts for certain offerings: ox, lamb, bird—down to grain, oil, and milk. Sometimes the offering would be burned, for only the god to enjoy. Other sacrifices would be divided among the worshippers as a way of uniting the community and sharing in the god's blessings.

Death and the Afterlife

We know very little about what the Phoenicians saw at the end of the road. Evidently they believed in some form of life after death, for they buried things with the dead person: ceramic vessels, food, glass vases, jewelry, weapons, toys, tools, and other personal items that would be wanted in a future life. But without written clues to the Phoenicians' beliefs, scholars can only guess.

In Sidon, wealthy parents presented this marble statue to the god Eshmun as thanks for healing their sick child. Made in the fifth century B.C.E., the statue shows the influence of Greek art.

The Phoenicians seem to have had a general idea of a shadowy underworld presided over by a deity called Mot ("death"), where the souls, or "shades," of the dead stayed. Messages engraved on tombs warned against violating the burial within, promising unpleasant consequences, but revealed little or nothing about the supposed fate of the dead person. What a contrast between these seemingly vague ideas and the Egyptians' firm beliefs in an afterlife and the elaborate preparations they made for the next world!

Another puzzle is that the Phoenicians and Carthaginians used both burial and cremation, even at the same time. Members of the nobility and wealthy people were buried in large sarcophagi placed in shafts cut very deep in the rock. Some of these astonishing excavations can be seen today at Byblos and Carthage. Cremated, or burned, remains were put in small stone boxes, sometimes placed in the same burial shafts with bodies. But if objects and protective amulets were included in the burials

This glass necklace was found on Sardinia, an island off the coast of Italy that was settled by the Phoenicians.

and not with the cremated dead, what does that say about belief in an afterlife? Maybe most Phoenicians felt that they should enjoy their lives in the here and now, because they couldn't be sure of much else later on.

⟞THE CARTHAGINIANS⟝

People in the western colonies, especially the Carthaginians, apparently were even more focused on religion than those in the home country. Scholars know more about what they did, at any rate, from reports by the Greeks and from archaeological discoveries.

Eshmun appears to have been the chief god in Carthage, along with Melqart, the god of the mother city, Tyre. Baal-Hammon was also important. In Carthage, however, it appears that Baal took on a character different from the way he was usually thought of in Phoenicia. Instead of a young man who personified nature, he seems to have become a more distant god, important in funerary ceremonies. The other most prominent deity was the goddess Tanit (tah-NEET). Possibly she was the same as Astarte, but scholars are not sure. Not only did she have the image of the mother goddess, with power over love, fruit, the moon, and the sea, but like Baal-Hammon she had an important funerary role. Inscriptions on Carthaginian stelae are always addressed to either Baal-Hammon or Tanit.

Many personal objects such as pottery vessels, jewelry, amulets, decorated ostrich eggshells, and ceremonial razors have been found in Carthaginian burials. These objects give us our few glimpses of the human beings who lived in Punic Carthage and what was important to them. Most touching of all are the small pottery containers, in the shape of a cow or a human head, with a hole on top and a smaller one where the mouth is . . . believed to be feeding bottles for babies.

Objects found in Carthaginian tombs—a box for cosmetics and a ceramic baby feeding bottle—give a glimpse of life in ancient times.

CHAPTER FOUR

OLD STORIES— AND SOME NEW IDEAS

Phoenician gods seem rather a shadowy lot. If monumental statues were made of them, like those of the Egyptian and Greek gods, they have not survived or have yet to be discovered. Aside from a few stelae, rather crudely carved, there are not many clues to the gods' supposed appearance. One type of figurine—many have been found at Byblos—is said to represent a deity, possibly Baal. It's a striding male, elongated and skinny, usually made of bronze and overlaid with gold leaf. Melqart and

A silent company of votive figurines. Sometime between the tenth and sixth centuries B.C.E., worshippers placed them in a temple at Byblos.

Could this be Astarte? We do know that it is a Phoenician ivory carving, showing Egyptian influence, made sometime between the tenth and sixth centuries B.C.E.

lesser gods were sometimes shown on the coins of Tyre. But as for the beauty of Astarte, the goddess of love, we can only imagine.

Baal and Adonis

In Canaanite times Baal, the young god who personified the growing season, inspired colorful myths. When vegetation died in the hot, dry summers, people said that Baal was dead and had descended to the underworld. Then, when the autumn rains restored life to the land, Baal returned in full vigor. Myths from Ugarit tell this familiar story of the ongoing struggle between fertility of the land, symbolized by Baal, and drought, personified by the god of death, Mot.

As for Phoenician times, because of the loss of any written material about religion, scholars can only guess whether the same sort of beliefs about Baal continued. But an echo may be found in Byblos. A Greek writer named Lucian visited Byblos in the first century c.e. and learned about a custom that the people still followed with great devotion. At that time the young god of the city was called Adonis, a word that, like Baal, means "lord."

Lucian reported that every year—it seems likely to have been in the spring—the women mourned the death of Adonis. At that time of year a

APHRODITE AND ADONIS

The Greek and Roman myth about the goddess of love and her lover, Adonis, is well known today. In fact, we still call a very handsome man an "adonis." This is the story that had its roots in the slopes of Mount Lebanon and the ancient seaside town of Byblos.

Adonis was a young man so beautiful that even goddesses could not resist him.

When Persephone, queen of the underworld, first saw him as a child, she was so entranced that she longed to keep him with her. But it was Aphrodite, goddess of love, who won the heart of Adonis. The two spent rapturous hours high on the mountainside, near a large spring today called Afqa, where torrents of sparkling water gush from a cave.

Adonis was a skillful hunter and frequently went off by himself in search of game. One spring day, however, a wild boar gored him in the side, and before Aphrodite could find him, he died. His blood turned to crimson the anemone flowers that covered the mountain slopes—and reddened the stream that flowed from the spring. Aphrodite mourned bitterly . . . but at last Persephone had *her* chance.

The story of Adonis, the young god who personifies fruitful nature, is found in other forms and other cultures of the ancient Middle East. Reflecting the long-lasting ties between Byblos and Egypt, it also echoes the story of Isis and Osiris, in which Isis seeks her dead husband. Centuries later, William Shakespeare told the story in a long poem, *Venus and Adonis*. It was his first work to be published—and made him an instant success!

river near Byblos, then called the Adonis River, ran a reddish color, which the people said was the blood of Adonis. (Lucian added that he talked with a more down-to-earth individual who said that the color came from the reddish soil of the mountains—which is actually rich in iron.) In any case, much weeping and wailing and tearing of hair went on, and the women made images of the god, which they threw into the sea. Then, said Lucian, after the people had had enough of beating themselves and lamenting, they made a funeral sacrifice to Adonis.

The next day the people rejoiced. Adonis, they said, had come to life again, and everyone was happy! Perhaps this was their way of reassuring themselves that the earth would indeed once more produce its fruits.

Phoenician Gods in Israel

Other clues about the effects of religion in the Phoenicians' lives come from books of the Old Testament. At times many of the people of Israel became interested in the Phoenician gods, with their strong personalities. Many wanted to follow the Phoenician cults, the emotionally exciting rituals based on fertility rites and nature worship. The Hebrew prophets denounced the "false gods" and urged their people to have nothing to do with the pagan rites.

The well-known story of Jezebel gives an idea of the tensions between the two very different religions of the Phoenicians and the Hebrews. Jezebel, who lived in the ninth century B.C.E., was the beautiful daughter of the king of Tyre. To further friendly relations between the two peoples, she was married to Ahab, son of the king of Israel. But good relations were soon marred by religion.

Not only did Jezebel want to worship Baal and Melqart in her new home, but she determined to make others follow the Phoenician religion. When he became king, Ahab went along with her, and Jezebel had shrines and altars set up wherever possible. The Hebrew prophets grew alarmed and condemned the pagan Phoenician religion. Finally, in a political revolution, Jezebel came to a bloody end. The Phoenician temples that had been built in Israel were destroyed, altars broken, sacred groves in high places cut down, and Baal's priests killed.

Thus Israel escaped the threat presented by the alien gods. But the violent conclusion of Jezebel's rule also had dire political results, for the

The beautiful, strong-minded Tyrian princess Jezebel, as imagined by a nineteenth-century painter, John Byam Liston

two-hundred-year alliance between Israel and the Phoenicians also came to an end. No longer could they work together in the highly profitable trade ventures they had undertaken jointly for so long. Furthermore, by splitting up, they were no longer strong enough to resist the aggressive conquerors from Mesopotamia: Assyria and Babylon. Religion had shown its power for destruction.

Child Sacrifice—True or Not?

Since ancient times people have believed that the Phoenicians—and even more so, the Carthaginians—practiced a horrifying rite: sacrifice of young children to the gods. Because this is one of the things that "everyone knows" about the Phoenicians, and a particularly sensational subject, we must give it some attention. First let's consider what "everyone knows."

The Hebrew prophets aimed their sharpest criticism at what seems to have been a Phoenician practice of child sacrifice. The Old Testament contains several warnings against "passing sons and daughters through fire," which certainly sounds like sacrificial burning of children.

In Carthage child sacrifice appears to have been a well-established practice. A Greek historian of the first century B.C.E. wrote a lurid account of the sacrifices, describing the fiery deaths of infants and young children offered by their parents to Baal-Hammon and Tanit. The charred bones of each sacrifice were put in a small pot and buried in a special place, with a stele commemorating the offering.

In the 1920s archaeologists excavated a place in Carthage that appears to be proof positive of this practice. It an area known today as the Tophet, thousands of small pots containing tiny burned human bones were unearthed. Many thousands more are estimated to be hidden under the houses of the modern town. The interpretation of this evidence, however, has raised much controversy. Some scholars believe that child sacrifices were held only in times of danger, when the Carthaginians believed they must carry out extreme measures to win the gods' support. The most notorious example took place in 310 B.C.E., when a Greek army came close to attacking Carthage itself. Fearing that the gods must be angry with them, the Carthaginians decided to sacrifice around three hundred children, some as old as twelve.

Other researchers have concluded that the sacrifices were carried on

Stelae in the Tophet of Carthage . . . do they represent sacrifice of children, or merely burials?

steadily, not just in times of danger. Whereas in the early centuries of Carthage, only the leading families were entitled to make this sacrifice as a privilege, later on people from all social classes practiced it—right up until the destruction of Carthage by the Romans. Some scholars have suggested that child sacrifice could even have been a form of population control. Other Punic colonies also appear to have followed the practice. Places like the Tophet of Carthage have been found at a town that is now Sousse, Tunisia, and at sites on Sardinia and Sicily.

The truth, however, may be totally different. Today some scholars reject the idea that the Phoenicians practiced child sacrifice. The biblical warnings against "passing through fire," they say, meant something else. As we have seen, the Phoenicians and

Carthaginians practiced cremation of the dead. The Hebrews opposed the practice of cremation; they believed only in burial. Therefore the prophets may have been warning their people not to follow the Phoenician custom of cremating the dead, particularly young children. Another possible explanation is that "passing through fire" meant dedicating the young person to a pagan god and bringing up that child in an alien religion.

Is there any archaeological evidence in the Phoenician homeland, one way or another? The answer is no—no site has ever been found that was clearly a place for human sacrifice. A flurry of archaeological excitement arose in 1991 when a large number of ancient jars were discovered buried in Tyre. They contained burned human bones—and it looked as though that site might indeed have been a "Tophet" for sacrifice. But when archaeologists examined the jars more closely, they decided that the bones were cremated remains from people of all ages, not just children. The site appears to have been a cemetery, therefore, not a sacrificial area.

But what about the Tophet in Carthage? The scholars who reject the idea that this was a sacrificial site believe that these thousands of burials were of infants who died at birth or soon afterward, because infant mortality was so high. These children were cremated and buried in a special place because, according to this view, they were too young to have become a part of their society. The inscriptions on the stelae refer only to a vow or a request for blessings from the god—not to sacrifice.

If this is so, then why did people claim that the Carthaginians sacrificed their children? We must remember that no written records by either the Phoenicians or the Carthaginians survived. Almost everything written about them in ancient times came from their competitors and enemies. The Hebrew prophets wanted to discredit the Phoenician religion so that their own people would not be attracted to it, and the Greeks wanted to make their enemies look bad.

Furthermore, the Greeks, like the Hebrews, did not practice cremation of ordinary people. They reserved cremation only for dead heroes, as a great honor. When they learned of the Carthaginians cremating young children, the argument goes, they were so shocked and disgusted that they decided it must be a matter of child sacrifice—rather than the burning of children who had died of natural causes. While some scholars who hold this view suggest that sacrifice of children could have taken place under conditions of great stress, they believe it was very rare.

IF YOU LIVED IN PHOENICIA

If you had been born in Tyre around 900 B.C.E., your way of life would have been determined by the facts of your birth—whether you were a girl or a boy, wealthy or poor. With this chart you can trace the course your life might have taken if you were a member of a high court official's family.

You were born in Tyre. . . .

As a Boy . . .   As a Girl . . .

You live in a narrow three-story house built of yellow stone. The houses are too close together to have a garden, but a few palm trees offer some greenery. Inside the high, thick walls that surround the small island city of Tyre, there's little open space other than the public plaza and marketplace. Besides fine carpets, your home contains only the necessary furniture: beds, stools, small tables, large chests. But they are all made of fragrant cedarwood, and some are trimmed with carved ivory. Your father is frequently away on diplomatic missions, and your mother dotes on you but leaves much of your care to her servants and slaves.

At age 8, preparing to follow your father's career, you attend a scribe school at the Temple of Melqart. Sometimes you're late to school because it's so interesting to linger by the crafts workshops and watch the artisans making things of gold, ivory, and blown glass. And sometimes you sneak off for a quick swim in the warm sea.

At age 15, you start accompanying your father on some of his missions, carrying messages between the king of Tyre and kings in distant lands. You're awed by the grandeur of the Egyptian temples—and proud of the temple in Jerusalem built by Tyrian stonemasons and artisans.

At age 20, in a simple ceremony you marry a girl from a similar aristocratic family, as arranged by the two families. Your father has purchased a house for you, to which you will add another story or two when the gods give you children.

At age 30, as the king's representative you are well rewarded for your services—a fine purple robe, gold and jewelry. But traveling such long distances and sometimes dealing with threats and the danger of bandits makes for a stressful life.

At age 8, you are no longer so free to watch the excitement of ships coming and going in the harbors, with your brothers and friends. You must start to learn household arts from your mother and her servants, especially spinning and weaving.

At age 15, you are married to a merchant, owner of several ships that trade with the Aegean Islands and Egypt. You look forward to a comfortable life in a fine house.

At age 20, the gods have granted you two sons, who will be raised to follow in their father's footsteps and become merchants.

At age 30, you and your husband frequently entertain other prominent merchants and persons close to the court. Your Syrian slave dresses your long black hair, and you are still known for your beauty. You enjoy wearing your ankle-length straight gowns of fine Egyptian linen and your delicate gold jewelry.

In old age, you are well cared for by your sons. At your death you are buried in a shaft or cave dug into the rock of the mainland. A few bowls and provisions, with personal objects such as your jewelry and personal seal, will be included to help you in whatever afterlife awaits you.

Who is right? The question of whether the Phoenicians and Carthaginians practiced child sacrifice is still very controversial. At the least, it is a warning that we can't believe everything we read about other people—especially if they can't speak for themselves. The source of the information may make all the difference.

How the Greeks Viewed the Phoenicians

The Greeks had very mixed feelings about the Phoenicians. On the one hand, their own culture was much less advanced at the time Phoenician culture was at its height, and they were greatly impressed. The Phoenicians appeared to be so clever, industrious, talented, and sophisticated, and they were such excellent seamen. If they occasionally were said to do bad things, such as kidnapping people into slavery, the overall picture was still decidedly favorable. Some scholars say that belief in certain Greek deities, such as Aphrodite, Dionysus, and Hercules, was originally inspired by the Phoenician gods. And everyone agrees that the Greeks learned about the alphabet from the Phoenicians.

But as the Greeks grew in confidence, during the first millennium B.C.E., they became fierce competitors with the Phoenicians. Then their attitudes changed. Admiration turned to suspicion and anger. Moreover, the Phoenician cities sometimes played a hostile role against Greece. Considering the importance of the Phoenician navies in the Persians' long and bitter campaign against Greece, it's no wonder that the Greeks had little love for the people they had earlier admired. Later, having taken over the Levant under Alexander the Great, the Greeks seem to have put an end to this rivalry by absorbing the Phoenicians into the Greek world.

In the next few hundred years, Phoenician culture faded. Because we know so little about them from their own words, the Phoenicians remain mysterious, elusive, hard to understand. Yet the land remained unchanged, and it continued to shape the people in certain ways. When we look at Lebanon today, some ideas that we have about the Phoenicians still ring strikingly true.

CHAPTER FIVE

PHOENICIANS IN THE MODERN WORLD

The alphabet takes first place among the Phoenicians' contributions to the world. Those busy traders and merchants, who needed a convenient way to keep their records, did everyone a huge favor. Within a few hundred years the alphabet was spreading throughout the Mediterranean world and parts of Europe, Asia, and Africa. Different languages had to have different signs devised for their own needs, of course, but the basics were the same. We owe the Phoenicians thanks for every book, advertisement, road sign, cereal package, report card, or whatever we read.

Special thanks go to Byblos. In ancient times, when it was called Gebal (a name close to its present name in Arabic, Jebeil), this prosperous town imported large amounts of papyrus from Egypt. Some of the papyrus was for its own record keeping, but a lot was then exported to other countries, especially Greece. The Greeks came to call the Phoenician town after the material itself: the name Byblos comes from the word "papyrus." In time the word Byblos stood for anything to do with writing and books. In English we have such words as bibliography, bibliophile (someone who loves books), and not least of all—Bible!

What else of their own invention or skills did the Phoenicians leave as their heritage? Decorative glassware,

Modern Beirut, with its rocky coastline

fine metalwork, and other artistic creations such as ivory carvings contributed to human beings' refinement and appreciation of beauty. Certainly, too, the reputation of Tyrian purple dye has enriched the world. Even if no ancient purple robes can be seen today, we still say such things as "born to the purple" for someone of aristocratic birth.

Phoenician seafarers were famous for their skill and courage in

exploring uncharted waters. The sea was a fearsome place, full of real and imagined dangers. Yet two thousand years before Columbus set out to cross an unknown ocean, Phoenician sailors were venturing into the vast and stormy Atlantic. With their bravery and improvement of navigational skills, they wrote an important chapter in maritime history.

Echoes from Ancient Times

What about religion? Although the Phoenicians' religion bears little relevance for us today, as an expression of humankind's spiritual experience it made a contribution to world religion. Furthermore, by forcing the Israelites to defend their own beliefs in contrast with the pagan gods and customs, the Phoenician priests indirectly helped the growth of Judaic and, later, Christian thought.

Another intriguing possibility lies in the story of the death and rebirth of Adonis on the slopes of Mount Lebanon. Similar ideas are at the heart of Christianity: the sacrifice and resurrection of Jesus Christ. Perhaps this similarity was one reason why the people of the Phoenician homeland accepted Christianity readily. Later, many of those who lived on Mount Lebanon held on to their Christian beliefs persistently even when most of the populations around them became Muslim. Easter, the time of resurrection, is still the most celebrated event of the Lebanese Christians' religious year.

The ancient site associated with the story of Adonis, the spring called Afqa high in Mount Lebanon, still has special meaning. The Phoenician shrine has long since disappeared, and only ruins remain of a small Roman temple to Venus built on the same spot. But to this day, people go there and hang tokens on the trees that grow over the surging water beside the ruins. These votive offerings, such as ribbons or small articles of clothing, express wishes for good health, a baby, or some other personal need. Possibly the people who leave them still believe the place has some divine blessing.

Here's another faint echo of the past. The bronze figurines found in Byblos, and images of Phoenicians in Assyrian art, show men wearing conical hats. Today some elderly men in small Lebanese villages wear a traditional style of hat in the shape of a cone. Possibly there's a connection between that type of hat and the ancient style of headdress.

The persistence of fashion: similar headgear on a sixth-century B.C.E. Phoenician and a Lebanese villager some 2,500 years later

Today's "Phoenicians"

Probably the most striking echo of the days of Phoenician glory are the people of Lebanon today. While some Lebanese still like to emphasize their "Phoenician" heritage, most set that idea aside as a romantic, out-dated notion. Both Christians and Muslims consider themselves Arab, because they speak Arabic and share many aspects of culture with the other Arab countries of the region. Yet just as the Phoenician cities stood out among the neighboring societies, in some ways the people of Lebanon are distinct.

Lebanon's geographical location as a "crossroads" and its long cultural tradition of trading with both East and West help explain this. Another factor is religion. Lebanon is the only Arab country whose population includes a large proportion of Christians. Because of this, for centuries contacts have existed between the people of Lebanon and Christians of

STONES THAT SPEAK

During World War II, American soldiers wrote "Kilroy was here" wherever they went. Whoever Kilroy was, his name popped up in the most unexpected places. But scribbling graffiti to show that you were "here" is nothing new. People loved to do it in ancient times, too.

There's one place in Lebanon with truly awesome "graffiti." On the coast north of Beirut, high rocks rise over the spot where the Dog River meets the sea. Conquering armies have been leaving their calling cards on those cliffs for more than three thousand years. The custom probably started with Ramses II of Egypt, who left no fewer than three reminders of his visits in the thirteenth century B.C.E. Thereafter, most of the invaders who targeted the rich Phoenician cities carved large inscriptions in the rock. The Assyrians, Babylonians, Greeks, and Romans are all there, and medieval Arabs as well. There are even twentieth-century inscriptions, including a very fancy one by the French, who governed Lebanon from the 1920s until the early 1940s, and one by the British, whose troops were stationed in Lebanon during World War II.

Unfortunately, this amazing graffiti gallery is threatened by the need for speed in today's Lebanon. A highway now passes just below the rocks, and several of the ancient "Kilroys" have faded badly because of air pollution.

Other stone reminders of the past have been found in just the last few years. During the dreadful war that gripped Lebanon from 1975 to 1990, downtown Beirut, the very center of the capital, was almost completely destroyed. But before the rebuilding started, archaeologists were given a chance to see what was under the demolished buildings and streets.

From ancient records scholars had known that a city called Biruta existed as early as Canaanite times, but little or no archaeological trace had ever been found of the earliest city. As soon as they started digging, archaeologists from the American University of Beirut unearthed the first physical evidence of Canaanite and Phoenician Beirut. Now massive Canaanite walls can be seen, plus Phoenician fortifications in the form of a triple glacis—three high, steeply sloping walls, or banks, covered with round stones. Plans for reconstruction of the downtown area call for preserving some of these walls in an archaeological park.

It took the tragic destruction of modern Beirut to bring the most ancient Beirut to light.

This Phoenician glacis, a defensive slanting wall, was discovered in the heart of Beirut in 1993.

Europe. Christian priests from Mount Lebanon studied in Italy in the 1500s, and a century later, Lebanese merchants were doing a brisk trade in silk with European ports. When American Protestant missionaries went to Lebanon in the first half of the nineteenth century, they found people receptive to modern education. At first most were Christians, but before long, Muslims as well were attracted to modern education and new possibilities.

Then, in the last decades of the nineteenth century, the mountains of Lebanon produced an explosion of emigration. Just as the people of the Phoenician cities had ventured to trade in far places, the people of Lebanon set out from home—and for similar reasons.

In ancient times there was not enough land on the coast of Phoenicia for people to make a living from agriculture. Therefore they made the sea their highway to success and riches. In the nineteenth century there was not enough land in the rugged mountains of Lebanon for growing families to support themselves. Just like ancient Tyre, mountain villages had an "over-abundance of young men." Young men left their villages, boarded ships, and sailed to distant places where they hoped to have better chances in life. Many women did so, too! Soon colonies of Lebanese were thriving in Africa, Europe, North and South America, and Australia. Most, in the early years of emigration, were Christians, soon to be followed by Lebanese people of other religions.

Typically, these modern-day Phoenicians became merchants, working their way up from humble beginnings. In the United States most started out as peddlers. They trudged through cities and countryside with packs strapped to their backs. While they did not sell carved ivory panels and beds of cedarwood, as in ancient times, they did sell beautiful embroidery and objects made of mother-of-pearl and olive wood from Palestine.

In an amazingly short time, Lebanese emigrants were living and working hard in every state of the Union. Whenever a peddler and his family had earned enough money, they would buy a horse and wagon, and then a little store where they could settle down to business. Many made fortunes. Just as in the days of the Phoenician merchants, fine fabrics and

A twentieth-century grocery store belonging to a Lebanese or Syrian immigrant in Brooklyn, New York

clothing were one type of goods in which Lebanese merchants and manu-
facturers specialized, and still do.

Unlike the people of ancient times, the modern emigrants and their
children had many possibilities besides trade. Lebanese became famous in
the United States in fields as diverse as entertainment and medicine, science and the arts, restaurants and scholarship, public service and athletics.
True to their reputation for developing the first easy way to write, the
alphabet, some became well-known writers in the nineteenth and early
twentieth centuries. They led the Arab world in a literary reawakening.

The most famous of these Lebanese-American authors is Kahlil
Gibran, whose books offer a philosophy of peace, religious tolerance, and
love. The following selection is from *The Prophet*, Gibran's best known
work:

> *And a youth said, Speak to us of Friendship.*
> *And he answered, saying:*
> *. . . let your best be for your friend.*
> *If he must know the ebb of your tide, let him know its flood*
> *   also.*
> *For what is your friend that you should seek him with hours to*
> *   kill?*
> *Seek him always with hours to live.*
> *For it is his to fill your need, but not your emptiness.*
> *And in the sweetness of friendship let there be laughter, and*
> *   sharing of pleasures.*
> *For in the dew of little things the heart finds its morning and is*
> *   refreshed.*

"Phoenicia" Today

Lebanon plays a unique role today in the Mediterranean world and the
Middle East. The Phoenician cities were usually not oppressed by conquerors because they were useful. In the same way, Lebanon depends on the
respect of its neighbors because of its distinctive character and usefulness.

In spite of its very small size, Lebanon provides vital services for the
whole region: banking, trade, education, manufacturing, communication,

In a village high in the mountains of Lebanon, back in 1895, a scene something like this took place.

A woman named Kamila confronted her husband in their shabby sitting room. "I'm taking the children," she told him, "and going to America."

"So! How will you live?" he asked.

"Never mind, I shall make my way."

The man shrugged and said nothing more. Possibly in her heart Kamila wished that he would go with them and not break up the family. Though he was a poor excuse for a father, her two sons still needed him. But she was prepared to travel alone, with the four children.

What Kamila found when she reached Boston was discouraging. A small pocket of poor Lebanese and Syrians lived in a miserable corner of the city, among other poor ethnic groups. But Kamila lost no time in getting to work. Like most Lebanese immigrants, she chose the only work she could: peddling. Each day, while a neighbor watched the children, she strapped a heavy wooden pack on her back and trudged around the city and suburbs, selling small pieces of linen and lace.

Soon her younger son, aged twelve, started going to a public school. There he attracted the attention of a volunteer who tried to help immigrant families. The young woman had noticed his unusual drawing ability. This became his ticket out of the slums—and into the world of artists and literary figures among Boston's elite. The poor boy from a mountain village became one of America's most loved writers, Kahlil Gibran, author of *The Prophet* and many other books. All his life he praised his mother, who had made the

Kahlil Gibran arrived in the United States a penniless child and became one of America's best-loved writers

courageous move to the New World.

In some ways Kamila's story, like that of so many other emigrants from Lebanon, echoes the tradition of the ancient Phoenicians. She took a boat to the West, seeking a better life. In another way, though, she was different. Unlike the Phoenician women, whose stories were not preserved and have been lost in time, she could leave a mark in the world by acting for herself. And she was not unique. Many Lebanese women have come to America over the years. Even though often illiterate, in the early days, some came by themselves and struck out on their own. Sooner or later, they—or their children—found "gold" in whatever kinds of work and profession they chose.

agriculture, tourism, resorts, and shopping (still the place to go for luxury goods!) Although these services were severely damaged during the war fought in Lebanon from 1975 to 1990, they are being restored. In peaceful times Beirut harbor throbs with shipping. Other cities, including the ancient Phoenician cities of Tyre, Sidon, and Byblos, hum with the sounds of construction machinery and speeding cars. The downside, unfortunately, is that the more the Lebanese build, the less of their country's natural beauty and archaeological heritage can be preserved.

Lebanon no longer sells cedarwood. Over the centuries those legendary forests have been reduced to small groves of trees in just two or three places in the mountains. But the remaining trees are so magnificent that the cedar tree has been adopted as Lebanon's national symbol. It appears on the flag—and everywhere else possible.

The go-getter attitude of the Lebanese is as strong today in the Space Age as it was in the Iron Age. Not just in trade but in many other ways, the Lebanese are as vigorous as ever at putting to work their talents and ambition. Thus the people of Lebanon keep alive the tradition of the ancient Phoenicians and contribute—far more than their small numbers would suggest—to the modern world.

High in the mountains of Lebanon, this cedar tree has been growing for some five thousand years.

The Phoenicians: A Time Line

*3000 Trade between Gebal (Byblos) and early Egyptian kings

2000 Possible arrival of tribes from elsewhere, leading to development of Canaanite culture

LATE BRONZE AGE	START OF THE IRON AGE		
	1000	500	0 C.E.

1200 Arrival of mysterious "Sea Peoples," a time of destruction and change

1100 Beginning of Phoenician cities' prominence as independent merchant city-states

1000 Earliest known example of Phoenician alphabet

950 Good relations between Phoenicia and Israel, Tyre becomes the leading Phoenician city and maritime merchant power

875 First of several Assyrian campaigns to conquer the region; Phoenician cities pay tribute

814 Legendary date of founding of Carthage, North Africa

605 Start of Babylonian control of the region following decline of Assyrian empire

538 Persian empire's control over and partnership with Phoenician cities, after defeat of Babylonians

333 Alexander the Great's conquest of Tyre and incorporation of Phoenician cities into his empire

146 Defeat and destruction of Carthage by Rome in Third Punic War

1 Phoenician cities, with gradual decline of Phoenician culture, fully a part of the Greco-Roman world

*All dates are approximate.

GLOSSARY

amulet: a charm to protect against evil

annals: records of events, arranged by years

artisan: a skilled craftsperson who works in one of the finer crafts; a goldsmith, glassblower, and lace maker are some examples of artisans

Bronze Age: the period in human culture and technological progress that followed the Stone Age; it was characterized by metalworking in bronze (a combination of copper and tin); in the Middle East it lasted from around 3000 B.C.E. until around 1200 or 1100 B.C.E., and was followed by the Iron Age

causeway: a raised walkway, usually constructed over rough ground or shallow water

chaos: a state of complete disorder and confusion, in which nothing has form or organization

cistern: a large storage tank for water, usually built underground

deity: a god or goddess, a divine being

fertility: productiveness, ability to reproduce or support growth; it can refer to soil, animals, humans, even imagination!

funerary: having to do with death and burial

graffiti: informal writing, usually names and short sayings, on public surfaces such as walls

indigenous: native to a particular region

inscription: writing of a formal or ceremonial nature, often on stone

Iron Age: the first millennium B.C.E., when people learned how to smelt iron and use it in tools and industry; in the Middle East it was followed, around 300 B.C.E., by the Hellenistic period, so called because of the dominance of Greek culture

Levant: a modern name for the countries bordering the eastern Mediterranean; the word comes from the French for "rise" and refers to the sun rising in the east (the Levant is "the east" in relation to Europe)

mercenary: a soldier hired to fight for a country other than his own

middlemen: people who handle trade between the producers of goods and the buyers of those goods

millennium: a period of one thousand years, usually reckoned backward and forward from the time of Jesus Christ

mollusk: a shellfish, such as a snail or clam; mollusks have soft bodies with no backbones and are protected by their hard shells

motif: in art, a repeated design

navigation: the science of figuring out the position and course of ships

notables: the important people in a society

pagan: referring to belief in multiple deities, specifically a religion other than Judaism, Christianity, and Islam

papyrus: the first "paper," made in ancient Egypt from strips of the papyrus plant

parchment: a writing surface made from the specially prepared skin of sheep or goats

relief: a picture or design carved so that it stands out from a flat surface such as stone

sacrifice: the offering of something valuable as a form of worship

sarcophagus (*plural* sarcophagi)**:** a large coffin, usually made of stone, for the burial of a royal or wealthy person

Semitic: relating to the Semites, peoples of southwestern Asia including the Canaanites, Phoenicians, Hebrews, and Arabs

stele (*plural* stelae)**:** an upright stone, in appearance much like a grave-stone, with a funerary or commemorative inscription

stonemason: a skilled worker who cuts and trims stone blocks for building

tribute: money and goods that a society has to pay a conqueror to acknowledge submission or in return for protection

votive: expressing a vow or wish

FOR FURTHER READING

Charles-Picard, Gilbert, and Colette Charles-Picard. *Daily Life in Carthage: At the Time of Hannibal*. New York: Macmillan, 1961.

Gray, John. *The Canaanites*. New York: Praeger, 1964.

Harden, Donald. *The Phoenicians*. New York: Praeger, 1962.

Healey, John F. *The Early Alphabet*. London: British Museum, 1990.

Herm, Gerhard. *The Phoenicians: The Purple Empire of the Ancient World*. New York: William Morrow, 1975.

Hoerth, Alfred J., Gerald L. Mattingly, and Edwin M. Yamauchi, eds. *Peoples of the Old Testament World*. Grand Rapids, MI: Baker Books, 1996.

Moscati, Sabatino. *The World of the Phoenicians*. London: Weidenfeld and Nicolson, 1968.

Tarnowski, Wafa Stephan. *Dances with the Gods: Canaanite-Phoenician Myths and Legends Retold*. Nicosia, Cyprus: Rimal Publications, 1997.

ON-LINE INFORMATION*

Fradkin, Robert. *Evolution of Alphabets*.
[http://www.wam.umd.edu/~rfradkin/alphapage.html].
The Metropolitan Museum of Art. *Ancient Near Eastern Art*.
[http://www.metmuseum.org/collections/department.asp?dep=3].
Siren, Christopher B. *Canaanite/Urgaritic Mythology FAQ*.
[http://webster.unh.edu/~cbsiren/canaanite-faq.html]

*Websites change from time to time. For additional on-line information, check with the media specialist at your local library.

BIBLIOGRAPHY

Aubet, Maria-Eugenia. *The Phoenicians and the West: Politics, Colonies and Trade*. Cambridge, England: Cambridge University Press, 1993.

Baramki, Dimitri. *Phoenicia and the Phoenicians*. Beirut: Khayat's, 1961.

Beirut College for Women. *Beirut: Crossroads of Cultures*. Beirut: Librairie du Liban, 1970.

Brody, Aaron Jed. *"Each Man Cried Out to His God": The Specialized Religion of Canaanite and Phoenician Seafarers*. Atlanta: Scholars Press, 1998.

Bullitt, Orville H. *Phoenicia and Carthage: A Thousand Years to Oblivion*. Philadelphia: Dorrance and Co., 1978.

Frazer, James G. *The Golden Bough: A Study in Magic and Religion*. 1890. Reprint, New York: Crown Publishers, 1981.

Gibran, Jean, and Kahlil Gibran. *Kahlil Gibran: His Life and World*. Boston: New York Graphic Society, 1974.

Gibson, John. *Canaanite Myths and Legends*. Edinburgh: T. & T. Clark Ltd., 1977.

James, E. O. *The Ancient Gods*. New York: G. P. Putnam's Sons, 1960.

Jidejian, Nina. *Beirut through the Ages*. Beirut: Dar el-Machreq, 1973.

———. *Byblos through the Ages*. Beirut: Dar el-Machreq, 1968.

———. *Sidon through the Ages*. Beirut: Dar el-Machreq, 1971.

———. *Tyre through the Ages*. Beirut: Dar el-Machreq, 1969.

Katzenstein, H. Jacob. *The History of Tyre*. Jerusalem: Schocken Institute for Jewish Research, 1973.

Kuhrt, Amelie. *The Ancient Near East c. 3000–330 B.C.*, Vol. 2. London: Routledge, 1995.

Lipinski, E. *Studia Phoenicia V: Phoenicia and the East Mediterranean in the First Millenium B.C.* Leuven: Uitgeverij Peeters, 1987.

Soyez, Brigitte. *Byblos et la Fete des Adonies*. Leiden: E. J. Brill, 1977.

Tubb, Jonathan. *Canaanites*. Norman, OK: University of Oklahoma Press, 1998.

Ward, William A., ed. *The Role of the Phoenicians in the Interaction of Mediterranean Civilizations*. Beirut: American University of Beirut Press, 1968.

INDEX

Page numbers for illustrations are in boldface

ABOUT THE AUTHOR

"A story set in ancient Tyre captured my imagination as a child—I could just see the gleaming white stone of magnificent palaces, broad stairs, and city walls. Years later, as a student in Lebanon, I visited the real Tyre . . . "

A native of Massachusetts, with a degree in international relations from Harvard University, Elsa Marston started a lifelong attachment to the land of the Phoenicians by marrying a Lebanese man. Many of her published works are about the Middle East, such as *Lebanon: New Light in an Ancient Land; The Ancient Egyptians* (Cultures of the Past); *Women in the Middle East: Tradition and Change; Muhammad of Mecca, Prophet of Islam*, and numerous articles and stories. Elsa and her husband, Iliya Harik, professor emeritus at Indiana University, live in Bloomington, Indiana, and have three grown sons. Elsa enjoys tennis, hiking, music, and yearly trips to see family in Lebanon.